ROCKY

A Life Transformed

BY

Arnaldo Concepcion
and
Jinelle Remo

Table of Contents

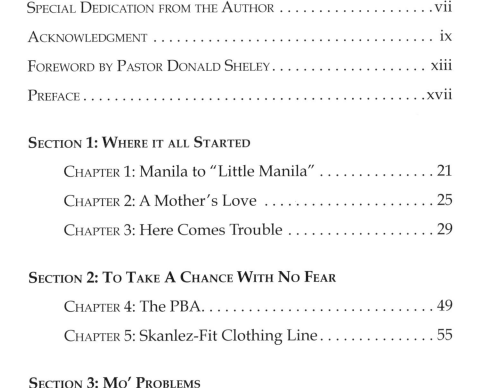

Special Dedication

I dedicate this book to my wife, Laura. Honey, thank you for loving me when I was at my worst. The worst is behind us now, but we have a long journey to go. I am blessed to take this journey we call life, together with you. God continues to use you to mold me into the man I am today. My prayer is to be able to love you as Christ loved His church, and that nothing, except God, will ever come between us. I love you and plan to love you for eternity!

To my children: Darien, Nathan, Neriah and Eliana. To Darien: this book pretty much tells the story of the hell I put you through. I know you've said you've forgiven me, but I want to express again how much I'm sorry to have put you through so much as a young boy. I am encouraged by the kind of man God is molding you to be. To Nathan: you are gifted in so many ways, and I know God will use you in a mighty way.

Last, but not least, to my twin daughters: Neriah and Eliana. By the time I started to write this book, you both were barely two-years-old. I was jobless, in my second year of college, and at home taking care of the both of you. You two are a Godsend and gave me the peace I needed each day. The four of you bring joy to my life. And your lives encourage me to never give up, no matter what — I LOVE YOU!

Acknowledgements

I've always wanted to write a book and I never thought that I would ever actually get around to it. One main reason why I could never begin writing was because of my inability in knowing how to write. It wasn't until I started my classes at Liberty University that I began to learn how to write and was encouraged to start writing this book. So, thank you Liberty University for "training champions for Christ."

Jinelle Remo, the co-author of this book, is a good friend and ninang (godmother) to my twin daughters. I started writing this book back in 2012, and was able to write more than half of it. But as I was about ¾ of the way through it, life became busy and I just wasn't able to write anymore. When I found out Jinelle was writing blogs, and I was finally able to read a few of them; that is when I prayed. Laura and I then got together with her to see if she might be interested in helping us write and finish the book. Jinelle, thank you for saying yes to this project. Without you, this book would probably never have been completed.

My parents, Armando Sr. and Myriam Concepcion; I drove down once a week from San Mateo to San Jose so they could spend time with the twins while I went to Starbucks or Barnes & Noble to focus on writing this book. Most of all, thank you for sharing stories with me that made it possible to have a good foundation for this book. I love you!

To the Church of the Highlands; you have made me feel at home and gave me a good foundation. For all the Pastors that mentored me through all the years since I've been there, ever since day one. Most of all, thank you Pastor Leighton for believing me, encouraging me and taking a chance with me.

Pastor Ted Melendez, a friend who tells you like it is. I always say, everyone needs a Ted in his or her life (like it or not)! You told me what I needed to know at the most crucial time, and because of that you've helped me grow into the person I am today. I love you brother, and thank you!

Alex Debniak. We've known each other for less than two years but we've had so many conversations, cried and prayed together that it seems like we've known each other forever. Thank you for choosing me as best man at your wedding; that really meant a lot to me. I thank God for putting you in my life.

My best friends Alex Catarroja and Matt Tinetti, for keeping me accountable and to never give up. What pulled me through my darkest moments were all your prayers and words of encouragement. Thank you for allowing me be real and comfortable with the man Christ has helped me become.

Last, but not least, my sister Emma. Every time I think through the stories of my past, it always reminds me how much you were always there for me. Whether it was my first 5150 hold, lying injured in the hospital or even visiting me in jail, you were always there to encourage and love me unconditionally. Even though I yelled at you during every visit, you never gave up on me. I love you so much!

There are many more people that encouraged and loved me that are not mentioned here, but you know who you are. My friends, family and even those behind the scenes that are always praying for me, thank you, and I love you!

Foreword

The Amplified Bible, 2 Corinthians 5:17 reads: "Therefore if any person is engrafted in Christ, the Messiah, he is a new creation, a new creature altogether. The old, previous moral and spiritual condition has passed away. Behold, the fresh and new has come." One of the thrills a Pastor enjoys is witnessing the change that is wrought when Christ begins His work in the life of a sinner. Paul calls it a "new creation."

The astronomer, Copernicus, was among the first to understand that the planet Earth was not the center of the universe, lent his name to what we call the "Copernicus Revolution" as a description of any kind of radical rethinking. The Apostle Paul is no less famous for his Damascus Road experience, which changed the whole direction of his life. Even though he was an outwardly religious man, everything previously had revolved around him. He had lived an egocentric life as the center of his own universe. He no longer lived for himself. He lived to please the One who loved him, who died and was raised again for him. Christ, not Paul, was the new center of Paul's universe: egocentricity had given way to Christo centricity!

While Paul's reference to a new creation summarizes the changes that occur within the life of any believer, these changes were dramatically focused within his own life.

Love was now the controlling motive in place of hate. Serving the One who died for him had taken the place of selfishness. True understanding of Jesus, His identity and achievement, replaced ignorance and error. The apostle's use of the vocabulary of the creation narratives in Genesis is striking. It is implied that unbelievers, as Paul had been, were blind and lived in darkness analogous to the primal darkness of the first verses of the book of Genesis.

Just as God spoke then and there was light; so too God speaks the gospel-word and once again there is light, though it is inward within the heart. By the agency of the Word of God, the message of reconciliation; people are remade.

In expressing the great and profound changes that occur in the life of anyone who is in Christ, Paul not only affirms that there is a "new covenant," there is also a new creation. The old has gone, the new has come.

When God was responding to Job's experience, He made the following observations: "Who is this that darkens counsel by words without knowledge? Dress for action like a man; I will question you and you make it known to Me. Where were you when I laid the foundations of the earth? Tell Me if you have understanding. Who determined its measurements – surely you know! Or who stretched out the line upon it? On what were its bases sunk or who laid its cornerstone when the morning stars sang together and all the sons of God shouted for joy (ESV)?"

The angels in heaven shouted for joy as they beheld God in the work of His creation of the earth. The Bible tells us that there is joy in heaven when one sinner repents. May I suggest that same joy fills the heart of the believer when he sees a new creation in salvation!

As you read the story of God's transforming work as it changed the life of the author of this book, your heart too will be filled with joy. Be ready to shout and praise God as you read this "new creation" testimony.

I know from first-hand experience…I am the Pastor who has observed this new work of creation.

Preface

August 9, 2006

I walked outside alone.

I wanted to explode with all the anger that had built up inside of me. I tried so hard to contain all my anger because lashing out always made things worse.

I'm tired of my life.

I'm tired of yelling at my wife, my children and my family. I need a way out, *permanently*. Just the thought of how many times I've disappointed them over and over again caused a stream of tears to pour down my face. The pounding in my chest gradually became louder with every thought of how much pain I've caused to the ones I love.

Somehow, the coldness and fog outside didn't seem to eliminate the burning emotions inside. This was my last suicide attempt; the one that I was confident would bring an end to my life. I'd always told my family and friends, "I'll never live to see my 30th birthday." Tonight was only seven months shy of my 30th birthday and I knew this was the very moment I had predicted.

However, I had never imagined that my life would end up this way. I had great ambitions to have a better future like the one my parents always talked about. Many of my dreams actually came true. Yet somehow along the way, the reality of my dreams started crumbling down as I began to fall apart with them. I thought I was a good person. Wasn't I? Or, maybe I used to be? Feeling more alone than ever, I looked up through the sheer blanket of fog and uttered the words of a dying man, "God, if you're there, please help me? I don't want to hurt myself; I don't want to hurt my wife or anyone else anymore. Please change me God?"

This was the end of my life.

What I didn't know was this very moment also marked the beginning of the life I was meant to have.

SECTION 1

WHERE IT ALL STARTED

CHAPTER 1

Manila to "Little Manila"

E very child anticipates living the care-free-stress-free-not-a worry-in-the-world kind of life. While that's the picture many children deserve, the truth is *that* kind of living is only experienced by a few. Broken families, with both parents working, and homes where children are left wondering when their parents will return home; shake the lives of these children. Regardless of these circumstances, most of the memories I have of growing up are great memories. Sure, our family had our struggles, but we also experienced a lot of enjoyable and uplifting moments.

Born in the Philippines to dad, Armando Sr. and mom, Myriam in 1977; I was the sixth child, but not the youngest. As many would expect, living in a house full of other kids to play with, it could get very chaotic. The house was full of laughter and occasionally, anger. But through our disagreements, our

family remained close. Although in the beginning, not everything was that way.

Kuya Tony

Kuya Tony resonates in my mind every year that passes by,
and I am reminded of him and the challenges that our family
faced. I will never fully understand what my parents and sister
went through. You see, after Ate (older sister in Tagalog) Lorna
was born, Kuya (older brother) Tony followed, but he had
health problems from the very beginning. I was told he spent
a majority of his time in and out of the hospital. And at the age
of one, he breathed his final breath. I don't know what it's like
to lose a child, especially at a young age, but I can't imagine
how difficult that experience was for my parents.

My parents never really talked about how the loss of Kuya
Tony affected their lives. But one day, I found the courage to
ask. Although their situation was very saddening, I'm glad
they persevered to have more children because I'd be without
my other older sisters Minda and Emma, without my Kuya
Armando Jr. and younger brother Niño. Niño's birth presented
another trial my parents and family had to overcome. Three
years after I was born, my brother Niño became part of the
family, though there were complications surrounding his birth.

My parents told me that when my mom was pregnant with Niño, the doctors suggested aborting the baby because the pregnancy would endanger her life. But, being a faithful woman, abortion was not an option for my mother. Looking back at the struggles surrounding my parents and siblings, I wonder how my parents kept such a positive outlook on life.

Sometimes it's nice to have a big family. Actually, being Filipino, even if you don't have a big immediate family, you'll always have a few cousins, aunts and uncles around. (Most times even when you refer to family members as "uncle" or "auntie," they're not even related to you by blood. That's just the type of relationship you've always had with them.) One of the greatest parts of having a big family is that there was always someone to talk to or hang out with, and there was never a dull moment…especially in my family.

However, having a big family like ours wasn't always easy, especially living in a third world country like the Philippines. My father, like many Filipinos, dreamed of one day moving his family to America, a land where his hopes and dreams (as well as the hopes and dreams of his children) could become a reality.

To make this dream our reality, my dad worked with a great deal of effort. He was a computer programmer for Philippine Airlines. Being mindful of his goal, along with hard work and determination, his dream came true. In 1982, my father accepted a job in San Francisco, and moved our family into a two-bedroom condo in Daly City, California...right next door to San Francisco.

Finally, my dad's dream, that we all had began to share, was becoming a reality, one that was going to bring us so much hope. And it did for most of us. But as for myself, I would see my hopes go down in flames. In fact, my parents said I had a horrible start before we even landed in the United States. They said I was so confused and terrified of the plane ride, I was actually screaming and trying to open the airplane door. This would be the beginning of my many tantrums that followed. But before we move too far ahead, let me tell you more about my family.

CHAPTER 2

A Mother's Love

Hearing the story of how my dad brought us to America always gave me encouragement. Being a hard working man, my father continued his work ethic in San Francisco. I always thought he could be the next Bill Gates or the Steve Jobs of his day, but he didn't want that kind of life. My dad always wanted a humble and simple life for himself and found happiness knowing that his family was taken care of. But of course, Dad wouldn't have been able to be successful in his work without my mom.

While my dad worked hard to put food on the table, someone had to cook it! I know everyone says their mom or grandma cooks the best Filipino food ever, but my mom is the BEST Filipino cook…hands down. With six growing kids running around, Mom had to be a good cook! Adobo, pancit, lumpia and her famous chicken wings would make anyone want to sit down and enjoy the love she poured into her food.

That's exactly what happened growing up. My friends often said, "We're going to Mom's house!" See, my mom didn't just show her love to her family, she expressed that same love to anyone who came over the house. That's why anyone who knew my mom called her "Mom." I didn't mind people calling her "Mom," especially if that meant having more food and friends around the house for us to enjoy!

It was natural that the love my parents had for those around them would be passed on among their children. This always reminds me of how much my parents love us. Even with the successful delivery of Niño, he still had complications growing up. He was always in special education classes because of his developmental disability. It was another struggle our family and I, but especially Niño, was able to overcome.

I remember a day when I was break dancing in the living room, and Niño and his friend asked, "Kuya, can you teach us how to dance like that?" Any other time, I probably would have said no, that I was too busy or maybe "How about another time?" But for some reason, I told my brother and his friend yes. That was when I found out my brother had a raw talent for break dancing!

Although Niño was struggling in school to learn at his grade level, he was able to learn break dancing moves quicker than I was able to. So, I decided to take him along whenever I went to house parties where there were break dancing battles. None of my friends ever knew or guessed about Niño's disability because of how quick he could learn on the dance floor. In less than a year, Niño became a better break dancer than me. It is another case where a student outmatches the teacher, but I didn't care because I was happy my brother found something that he really enjoyed.

I really admired how Niño fought against his disability, in more ways than just break dancing, but in every aspect of his life. When Niño reached the 7th grade, he was able to attend school in regular classes with everyone else. Today, Niño is managing a store for one of the largest mobile companies in the world, attending Phoenix University for a bachelor's degree in business and happily married to his wife. Niño may have learned a few dance moves from me, but he taught me how to keep pursuing my desires even when the odds were against me.

CHAPTER 3

Here Comes Trouble

Daly City, 1982

To fully understand my story, it's important to see that a lot of the trouble I got into literally started on my first day of school…in kindergarten. I was terrified for my first day! Going to a new school in a new country, while learning a new language, was not the easiest task for a 5-year old! Minda, Emma and Armando Jr. had an easier transition than I did, because they were able to learn and speak English back in the Philippines. However, I did not. Being that this would be the first time entering a formal American classroom, my father decided to give me one piece of advice: "Rocky, don't get into any fights on your first day of school." My dad quickly reminded me of why I got the name "Rocky" in the first place.

Back in Manila, my uncles and cousins would put boxing gloves on all the kids and teach them how to defend themselves.

In reality, no one wanted self-defense lessons; we just wanted to fight each other. Around the time when I was born, the movie *Rocky* starring Sylvester Stallone was a big hit in the Philippines. As a little kid, my family noticed I had pretty huge hands, so they decided 'Rocky' was an appropriate nickname for me. Little did they know that I would live up to that name.

When my father expressed a direct order, it was best to follow his directions. So, when he said not to fight on my first day of school, I made sure I did everything I could to respect his wishes. But that first day at Junipero Serra Elementary was extremely difficult! All those fears made it so impossible for me to leave my mom's side that the principal had to force me into the classroom. So here's 5 year old me, being carried into kindergarten class, kicking, screaming and swearing at the principal in Tagalog for making me go to school!

After a long episode of kicking and screaming, I somehow managed to calm down and hold on to some crayons until recess. Recess was another obstacle I would face. I was alone during recess with no friends to play with, a typical new kid's "first day at school" experience. Not knowing what to do, I decided to stand along the fence until recess was over, and hopefully avoid contact with anyone. However, the class bully had other plans in mind for me. He mocked and shoved me against the fence. The whole time I kept repeating to myself the words my father had said before school: "Don't get into a fight. Don't get into a fight." So I let the bully punch me until recess was over.

After three long hours of kindergarten, nothing made me happier than seeing my mom and baby Niño picking me up from school! Little did I know that my mom had never gone home after dropping me off for my first day! Maybe she sensed I'd needed her presence that day. And it turned out I actually did. That evening, I spoke to my dad about my classmate that had picked on me that morning.

My dad asked, "Well, what did you do?"

I answered, "I didn't fight like what you said."

Dad replied, "Good."

During recess the next morning, the same bully decided to pick on me again. After one shove from the kid, I retaliated by throwing a punch to his face that started our schoolyard fight. Actually, there wasn't much of a fight. One blow to the face and he knocked out pretty hard. Not surprisingly, I was sent to the principal's office and then waited for my father to pick me up from school. The angry look on my dad's face was not what I wanted to see this early in the morning.

Crossly he asked, "Why did you get into a fight?"

I answered, "Dad, it is not the first day anymore."

That probably wasn't the answer my father wanted to hear. Thankfully, other students told the principal that the bully had been picking on me since the first day of school. The principal decided to let me stay for the remainder of that day. So, I was off the hook, at least this time. But after that second day of school, trouble seemed to follow me wherever I went.

Daly City, 1986

The next time I found myself in trouble, a different kind of trouble, was in the fourth grade. One day after school, my friends decided to go to the Montgomery Ward store at Serramonte Mall. I wasn't sure why we decided to hang around there, until I saw my friends eyeing the GI Joe action figures. My friends convinced me to put one of the figures under my shirt and told me to walk outside the store and wait for them.

What I didn't see coming was an undercover security guard asking me to return back to the store! I was freaking out and had no idea what would happen. My two friends had gotten caught inside, but I was the only one who made it out of the store with the action figure. Like any other kid my age, my friends played the "blame game." Technically, it isn't considered stealing until you leave the store. I was blamed for the whole thing. Thankfully, the store manager didn't give me any penalty, but as I waited for my sister to pick me up, I knew I'd receive my discipline at home. All in all, my parents were *very* gracious.

Daly City, 1987-1990

There's a statistic that says moving to different schools, especially during elementary years, can have a negative effect on a child's intellectual and social development. Looking back at my life, I believe the second part of that statistic was very true. I attended kindergarten through fourth grade at Junipero Serra Elementary. When my family moved to the Daly City Mission District; I attended John F. Kennedy Elementary for fifth grade.

Unlike my previous school, the kids at JFK were a lot bigger than the kids at Junipero Serra. When I saw how big the kids were, I told my brother Niño that when the time came and I was one of the older kids in school in another year, he wouldn't have to worry about being bullied, because I'd be there to protect him. At our old school, since Niño had a difficult time learning, they had to place him in the special needs classes. Kids at the other school often made fun of special needs kids, including Niño. So, when we got to JFK, I wanted to make sure that no one bullied Niño like that again. The funny thing was JFK only went up to 5th grade, instead of 6th, like Junipero Serra. This meant the big kids I saw were in my grade, which would make me one of the older kids in school already.

On our first day, I wasn't too sure how well I would be able to protect myself, let alone Niño. But I knew enough back then, that I had to gain respect fast, so I wouldn't get bullied like on my first day in kindergarten. I searched for the biggest kid in school to fight, to earn respect. It turned out the biggest kid was the school bully. After I chose to fight him and won, he no longer messed with me or anyone else; and no one else dared to mess with me. I became somewhat of a hero to anyone who didn't like the school bully. Despite the "following" of people who respected me, there were still moments where I got into fights and lived up to the name "Rocky".

Well, I survived another year in another new school and now it was time to move again. I never truly understood the reasons we relocated so much, in such a short period, but it meant another new school for my brother and I. By this time, I was twelve years old and being the new student again, I was tired of fighting, so, I started looking for a different approach in making friends. I began to get involved in sports and that was when I met one of my good friends, DeAnthony Lowe, also known as "De." What was cool about De was that he loved sports and also loved to fight. It was great to hang out with a friend who did all the fighting for the both of us. De and I conveniently lived on the same block, separated by two houses. We were able to become really close friends and still are to this very day. DeAnthony also helped me get my first job…as a paperboy.

From a young age I began to enjoy making my own money. As early as the 2nd grade, I remember delivering food for my mom in the summer. Occasionally my mom would cook *lumpia, michado*, and *kare-kare* with her homemade *bagoong* for their coworkers. Of course everyone wanted her food, just like my friends craved it. When I accompanied my mom to work, I would offer to walk around the office building and deliver whatever she made, to her and my dad's co-workers. Since this took a lot of time, her co-workers were very kind to tip me, and even my mom would give me a few extra bucks for helping her out.

With that being said, I took advantage of the paper route to make substantially more money than I could by delivering homemade food. However, at the time I didn't have a bike to deliver papers. Delivering papers without a bike would have been a huge obstacle. My dad agreed to buy me a bike, if I agreed to pay him back right away from my earnings. Fortunately, paying him back took less time than I thought, and this made me very happy. Now, I could finally enjoy spending my pay on what I truly wanted. I spent most of my earnings on clothes, food, and bought my first bowling ball! The significant purchase of my first bowling ball will be important, but this would be more obvious later in my life.

Daly City, 1988

It wasn't until middle school that trouble decided to cut me some slack. I didn't have much of a choice anyway, as being involved in sports at Fernando Rivera Middle School meant I had to stay out of trouble to remain on the team. I assumed that being in sports would help keep me out of all that mess, but since gang violence was heavy in Daly City, especially around the late 1980's, I couldn't avoid the violence completely. Daly City was, and still is, heavily populated with Filipino immigrants. (I'm sure you've heard Daly City referred to as "Little Manila" or Serramonte mall as "Serramanila.")

Back in the day, Filipino gangs were roaming and ruling the streets throughout Daly City. There were stabbings and killings between the Filipino gangs who eventually went against gangs of different racial backgrounds. Most of the time, the Filipino gangs enjoyed fighting each other. Daly City in the late 80's and early 90's looked like the movie, "Colors" a film about the Bloods and Crips gangs of Los Angeles.

This may be a bit of an exaggeration, but a city mimicking that movie can make it a pretty dangerous place to live. Back then, if you walked around the main streets of Daly City wearing red, the Crips would mistake you as a rival gang member, and vice versa. But, then it got worse. If you weren't wearing red or blue, the Filipino gangs cruising around tried to pick on you to cause trouble.

One day, I was walking with a friend on Serramonte Blvd. in front of the old Serramonte Del Ray High School, when a car full of Filipinos pulled up beside us and pointed a shot gun at us. All that my friend and I could do was run and hide for our lives. Since that day, I've never walked on the main streets of Daly City. I've managed to get to where I need to go by taking side streets or even walking through people's yards to avoid any car slowing down near me. The funny thing about this is; I never told my parents because it would have meant I wouldn't be allowed to go out anymore. In fact, most of the stories in this book are probably the very first time that my parents will hear them. However, one story they do know and still remember happened in the summer before my 8th grade year.

In the summer of 1988, my sister was part of a karaoke band. She started performing in the bar at Classic Bowling Center, where my family spent a lot of time together bowling. A virgin strawberry daiquiri was my usual order during my sister's set. During one evening, she played at a Filipino restaurant (instead of Classic Bowl) that was near the 7-11 on Westborough Avenue. Unfortunately, I wasn't able to order my strawberry daiquiris at this particular restaurant. So, I decided to head over to 7-11 and buy chocolate milk.

It was around 1 a.m. and while I was inside, this guy asked me if I had money. I told him I only had enough for my drink. I paid for my drink and started to walk out. Instantly, as I began to step out of the door of the 7-11, I got punched right in the face and fell straight down to the ground. At this point, I felt my right cheek on the cold cement. Like a nightmare, I saw five other guys coming out of the car to throw in their own kicks and punches. It was now six against one. They picked me up and threw me down so many times that I somehow ended up in the middle divider on Callan Boulevard.

I thought it was never going to end, and at one point thought they were going to beat me until I was dead. All I could do was swing and kick my arms and legs, hoping I would make contact. I don't remember if I hit someone, or if they let me go, but somehow I got away and ran back to the restaurant and straight into the bathroom. While in the bath-room, all I could do was sit there…bleeding, scared and crying. When my brother-in-law Christian came into the bathroom, he looked shocked and asked me what happened. I told him a bunch of kids jumped me outside of the 7-11. Christian went to get my dad, who saw the condition that I was in and he became furious.

Dad asked me to go with him and his friends back to the 7-11 and point the kids out to him, so that they could confront them. Of course, I knew that my dad and his friends were going to retaliate against them. But when we were on our way there, I was fearful that because of this, I might one day cross their paths and maybe have to face something worse. So, out of this fear, I stayed across the street outside of the restaurant while my dad and his friends ran across. By the time they got to the 7-11 to confront the kids, they were gone.

Before that night I'd never seen my dad so angry that he considered taking revenge. While I don't agree with the idea of revenge, his reaction to what happened really showed how much he cared for me. You see, while I was growing up, my father and I were not the type to vocalize or express our feelings for each other. I always knew that he loved me and he knows I love him, but this specific night reminded me how much my father cares for his family. After that night, it was extremely difficult for me to trust anyone anymore. Looking back, what I learned from this tragic incident made me more aware of my surroundings and taught me to become more "street savvy."

Unfortunately, more events happened so that I feared I wouldn't even live to see high school. Now in 8th grade; four friends and I were walking to the store when a group of kids from Westmoor High School approached us. When they got closer they demanded that we take our jackets off. The jackets we wore were popular at the time, called parkas, with a sports team logo on them. When we didn't comply with the demand to take the jackets off, one of them pulled a gun from his pants and pointed it at us, threatening to shoot if we didn't hand the jackets over.

I really didn't want to give up my jacket because I worked so hard to make the money to buy it. Plus, I was a very stubborn person. However, it was not only my life that was in danger, but my friend's lives too. I had no other choice but to give up my jacket along with everyone else. Now, I think it was a smart move because we survived the situation. Little did we know that we would all end up going to the same school, with the same kids the following year. Even before I got to high school there was a lot of drama leading up to my freshman year.

In the summer before my freshman year at Westmoor, the Filipino gangs were still going strong. They were getting involved in even more violence against other gangs in Daly City. Gangs also showed interest in drugs, meth in particular. One evening during the summer, a Filipino gang was in a search of a young African American man from a different gang to take revenge on. They were all high on meth and were on a mission to kill this young man.

Unfortunately, because they were high, they blindly shot and killed the first black person they saw walking around that same neighborhood, and ended up killing the wrong person. Because of their mistake, this created a huge tension between the two cultures and started the gang violence between Filipino and black gangs. A few months later, I would attend Westmoor High School where I would personally witness this war.

Daly City, 1991

Talk about the anxieties of the first day of school; not only did I have to worry about social status and making friends, but I also had to worry about gangs. I remember walking through the quad and seeing all the clubs out there promoting how great your high school experience could be if you joined their club. Well, back then, gangs were scouting for people who could prove to be a useful member in their groups. As best as I could, I tried to keep under the radar from all the recruiters.

Since I was in a public school and gang violence had been increasing, it shouldn't have been surprising that a fight broke out during lunch on the first day of school. A big black guy threw a Filipino guy through a glass window. I didn't know the exact details of this fight, but I knew for sure it was retaliation from what happened a few months before. Before that day, I thought I was pretty safe since I had black friends like DeAnthony. However, the tension between the black and Filipino gangs was so strong, I was afraid that the color of my skin would make it unsafe for me at Westmoor. I had to make a choice at this point. The first choice I thought I had to make, was to join a gang myself or keep playing sports which would hopefully keep me out of trouble.

Sports were always a great outlet to keep me out of trouble. The only problem was my parents didn't want me to play tackle football for fear I would get badly injured. Initially, I wanted to play football because I loved the sport. Now, I was motivated to play football to stay out of trouble, and hopefully make new friends. Not to profile black people, but a majority of the football players at Westmoor were black, and they were the better players.

Growing up playing sports, I learned that your team-mates became your family. Therefore, my hope was to join the football family, a family that would stick up for each other. When I got home that night, I told my parents about the incident at school and pleaded with them to let me play football. They agreed, and I was able to make new friends, friends that became my family.

Now I began my high school career. Honestly, I had a great time at Westmoor High School. I was very involved in sports and other activities there. I didn't have a problem making friends and got along with everyone at school, even though I ran into a lot of trouble with teenagers from other schools. My first two years of high school were a breeze. I played on the basketball team and started as quarterback of our football team by my sophomore year. For some reason, I decided not to play football during my junior year. That's when I stumbled upon my first major problem at Westmoor.

I tried really hard to prevent trouble from following me, so of course sports were the main means to help me accomplish that goal. By this time in my life, like any other high school kid,

I became really interested in girls. But the only time anyone in high school could hang out with their significant other was after school — the same time as football practice.

Like most kids, I focused most of my time after school hanging out with my girlfriend. Since I wasn't involved with sports in my junior year, my attempts to force trouble out of my life were ineffective. I experienced your typical public school difficulties: cutting class, a couple of arguments, etc. Most of the major issues and threats against my life were all students from other schools assuming I was someone else! As you've seen before, situations like these never turn out well.

One Saturday afternoon, I attended a school friend's birthday party at Gellert Park in Daly City. During a game of basketball with my friends, I was confronted by three teenage strangers…triple my size! The next thing I knew, one guy started throwing punches to my face. The first thing I told myself was don't hit the floor, unlike the last time I was in this situation. Hitting the floor meant a beat down, and I definitely didn't want to experience that again.

After I was hit and shoved several times, I got away into my car and drove off. As I drove off, I tried to figure out what I'd done to these guys for them to give me a beat down? It turned out these guys mistook me for another Filipino guy that *supposedly* picked a fight with one of their family members.

"How lucky I was...not," I thought. And this wasn't the last time someone made this same mistake.

A few months later, I was about to walk to my high school gymnasium to watch a basketball tournament, when a stranger decided to point a gun directed at my stomach. Based on the pressure against my abdomen, I felt that he was committed to shooting me. In a matter of seconds, someone that knew *both* of us yelled out, *"That's not him, that's not him!"* I remained frozen until the gun was clearly pointed away from me. At the time, that was probably the closest I ever felt to death.

The same year, I became enemies with a guy from another school because his girlfriend was interested in me while they were together. For the record, I was *not* interested. Although that didn't matter to him, he was still convinced he had to do something about me. One night during a school dance, the guy from the other school brought his machete to the dance and swung it towards my head. I guess you could say I was lucky, as I had fast reflexes. Thankfully, some of my friends from the football team were there to tackle the guy and gave the police a chance to apprehend him.

I realized that many of the problems which occurred during my junior year could have been avoided had I remained involved in sports. So I made sure I got back into sports, and during the middle of the basketball season, I joined the team. That summer, I went back to playing football and basketball for my senior year. My senior year was amazing! Most of my friends took as many classes as they could to gain enough credits for graduation, while I cruised by with only three classes and more than enough credits to graduate.

So at this point, I've gotten beaten and held up at gun point more times than anyone should have at such a young age. Despite these physical beatings, I survived academically in high school. I didn't know it then, but all of those seemingly tiny messes prompted a list of future destructive behaviors that lead me to believe that taking my own life — *suicide* — was the cure for all the pain welling up inside me.

SECTION 2

TO TAKE A CHANCE WITH NO FEAR

CHAPTER 4

The PBA

Daly City, 1995.

Freedom! After years and years of homework, tests, and grades, I was finally done with high school. Even though I received decent grades at Westmoor and had fun, the only motivation for me to succeed was making my dad and mom happy. I always hated school and couldn't have been happier to graduate and finally move forward in starting my own life. Honestly, college wasn't even a thought in my mind.

Being a recent high school graduate, I knew I'd have to start at the bottom of the workforce and strive hard to move up into the coveted jobs of society. I worked, worked and worked almost every job you can think of. My jobs ranged from a Burlington Coat Factory men's department manager to a cook at Joe's Cable Car Burgers, and front desk operator/ special events coordinator at Classic Bowling Center.

Having all this work experience was gratifying, especially when employed at Classic Bowl. Bowling was an activity that my family and I enjoyed together when I was younger. At thirteen, I bowled a perfect game (*yeah…I get lucky once in a while*). Anyway, my father saw that I had a natural talent for bowling. So when I opted out of college, he introduced me to amateur bowling tournaments so I could make a little extra money on the side. And my very first bowling ball purchase was going to make a huge impact on my life.

After I'd been bowling for about a year, my girlfriend at the time told me some news that would change my life. At nineteen years old, I was going to be a father. *How can I be a father when I barely started to live my life?* Like any other person at nineteen, I freaked out for a bit…wondering how I could possibly be ready to be a dad. I was more scared about how my family would feel, especially my older brother.

I always looked up to him, and now getting ready to be a young father — I thought he would be mad at me, and tell me how stupid and irresponsible I was. I was scared to tell anyone. But my brother was the one I knew I needed to talk to first, as he would give me the best advice. So when I finally got the courage to tell him, I was surprised. What I thought was going to be a long and painful lecture, actually turned out to be very encouraging. My brother was so loving and supportive, and the conversation we had that day actually gave me the confidence I needed to be the best father I could be. But I knew my life was about to change.

What would I have to sacrifice in order to be a dependable father? But then, I stopped for a moment and realized that I'd have the chance to be one of the greatest role models in my child's life. I was overjoyed when I found out that we were having a son! I still remember when I told my friend Greg that I was having a boy. We were both so excited that it felt like we almost broke the bones in our hands when we gave each other high fives.

Although I still had my doubts about being a responsible father, I looked forward to the life I would share with my kid. In December 1996, my first son Darien finally became real and a part of our lives. I was overjoyed. I was so worried about being a father that I couldn't imagine everything would actually be okay. However, I knew I had to provide a great life for my family, the same way my father had done for us. That's when I realized that bowling could be used as a source of income.

While I had natural talent for bowling, it was crucial to develop my skills further when going against tough competitors. I constantly sought out others who were very talented, mature and good role models in the sport of bowling. From the time I found out I was going to be a father; I started to win or place in the top 5 in almost every tournament I entered. In fact, I won so many handicap tournaments in Northern California that I exhausted all my handicaps and was forced to travel down south.

That was when my coach and friend introduced me to tournaments like ABTA (Amateurs Bowlers Tour) in Southern California. Ironically, I took 2nd place the first time I played in the tournament, and won a lot of money playing other tournaments the same weekend. However, my success in the sport did not end there. During this time period, I had the opportunity to travel between Alabama, New Mexico and Nevada to compete on a national level. These players were tougher and challenged me to play better than ever. More importantly, Darien was a constant reminder that all the hours I spent bowling were more than just what place I was in, but how well I could provide for my family.

It wasn't until July 22nd, 2001, that I reached my greatest personal accomplishment in bowling. By this time, I had become part of the Professional Bowlers Association (PBA). What that meant was the competition was superior to any other I'd encountered before. On that day at Earl Anthony Bowl in Dublin, California, I shot a *perfect game*. The difference between this game and the rest was that this achievement was accomplished at a professional level. Even nowadays, few can truly describe the feeling of attaining that level of success and have a ring to prove it. Honestly, making money in the PBA was very difficult, but it was an experience I really enjoyed. And the money I made from bowling was enough to support my family. Also, it gave me an opportunity to pursue another dream.

CHAPTER 5

Skanlez-Fit Clothing Line

Daly City, 2000

There were two aspects of my life that I knew, when put together, big things would happen. 1) My ability to formulate new ideas; and 2) My power of persuasion (hence, why I landed various sales associate jobs). With the extra money made from bowling, I pursued the idea of creating my own clothing line called "Skanlez-Fit." Around this time, big clothing brands like FUBU had inspired San Francisco Bay Area clothing lines to create attire that urban youth wanted to wear. Like a chain reaction, the brand "Suckafree" by Alfred David and "Buckwild Gear" by Keith Okada came about, which then inspired my own clothing brand.

When figuring out a name, I wanted the title of my brand to speak about who I was around this time. Despite my success, between a new family and bowling, I was still a twenty-three year old punk who got into a few conflicts once in a while. The term *skanlez* meant "to take a chance with no fear." I applied that mindset to my bowling career, family and social life.

Six months into the business, Skanlez was sold at 12 retail stores and became a very well known brand in the San Francisco Bay Area. Personally, one of my biggest supporters, aside from family and friends, seemed to be radio disc jockey Chuey Gomez (who is currently at HOT 105.7 and HOT 100.7). He made references to Skanlez when he aired on the station, and wore a Skanlez shirt several times a week during his show, California Music Channel (CMC).

Skanlez-Fit even made an appearance on a music video by rap star Money B ft. Yuckmouf from the Luniz! This whole experience of success seemed surreal. Winning tourneys weekend after weekend, and the growth of my clothing line felt exhilarating. Unfortunately, with every high in life, there's always that momentary low point.

Between bowling and a new startup company, it wasn't a surprise that I neglected my girlfriend, Darien and now a second son, Nathan. There's a saying, "distance makes the heart grow fonder." Well, distance seemed to make the heart grow indifferent. Between training for tournaments and promoting Skanlez-Fit, I wanted to focus all my time on those aspects of my life and was willing to sacrifice my time with Darien and Nathan. Because of everything I chose over my family, the relationship between my children's mother and I could not continue. Once that momentary low started, my life turned for the worse and it seemed like my life would remain in that low for a very long time.

SECTION 3

MO' PROBLEMS

"Finding relief in your problem is fine, but it will not cure the problem."

Henry Brandt

CHAPTER 6

When Trouble Stayed

I'd liked to say that all this success started the trouble that stayed with me the next few years. But truthfully, trouble rooted itself when I was arrested at 18 years old. In 1995, I committed credit card fraud that totaled over $10,000. I was looking at a hefty jail sentence and a felony charge on my record. Thankfully, the cops and the store where I made the purchases gave me a chance to return the items bought with the credit card, and my lawyer got my sentence lowered to a misdemeanor. However, one arrest was not enough to keep me at bay with my poor choices.

Like any other kid out of high school, I was desperate for money. So I began to sell various types of drugs such as: marijuana, ecstasy, Vicodin and methamphetamine. I typically used whatever drug I was selling at the time. Except, when I first tried meth, I hated it. *(But I never expected I'd come across the substance later in life.)* Truthfully, my "drug problem" had not even developed until after Darien was born. And of course, I also began to drink during my early high school years.

As I mentioned before, to really understand how I got to the night of August 9th, 2006, one has to understand that all these *seemingly* typical teenage issues amplified themselves into a problem I felt incapable of handling. My first suicide attempt was in 1997. I found a bottle of painkillers and swallowed the entire contents of the bottle (around 30+ pills). Had my friends Barry and Damond not found me on the floor that day; I'm not sure what would've happened to me. I was disappointed that this first attempt was a failure, so I made sure the second attempt would be successful.

In 1999, I got a hold of a HK-45 that would fire for sure, no problem. So here was my second chance at attempted suicide, this time I pointed the gun directly at myself. *Deep breath.* Gun pointed to my head and I pulled the trigger…nothing. I was sure the gun was completely loaded, so what happened? The barrel jammed. I took this as a sign that I had another chance at life and decided to take advantage of this reprieve. However, I was still frustrated and angry that my second attempt was unsuccessful. So I threw the gun down and held off making other suicide attempts for two more years.

CHAPTER 7

Relentless Rebellion

Daly City, 2000

With all of the successes from bowling and Skanlez-Fit, I got heavily involved with gambling. I frequently made trips to Reno and Las Vegas, spending hours playing roulette and craps. Anyone who gambles knows that putting up money in these games contains a certain amount of risk. I wasn't afraid of taking these risks. Greediness had taken a strong grip on my life and I made *zero* attempts fighting against it. When I wasn't able to make trips out to the casinos, I made bets on football games.

Most people who gambled on football games know this was easy money, as long as you knew who to bet for. What was unfortunate for me was that football was seasonal, so during the off-season I had to find other sports to bet against. At the time, I placed bets on basketball and baseball games. That wasn't a good sign. Betting on basketball and baseball games is usually a sign of desperation, as games occur almost every day, whereas football was about once a week. What I wasn't able to see was the danger I not only placed myself in because of gambling, but also my family.

My family. The choices I had made caused me to believe that my sons deserved someone better than me as their father. Darien and Nathan (at the time 5 years old and 8 months old respectively) would have a better life if I weren't around. In 2001, I made my 3rd suicide attempt. *"Maybe 30 pills weren't enough, better swallow more just to be sure,"* I thought to myself. I also took further precautions so that no one would find me. I swallowed over 100 pills, went into my black Cadillac Escalade, drove into the night and parked at a school parking lot while I hoped the pills took their toll on my body. Little did I know my family called Daly City police and searched everywhere for my location. After a few hours and no luck ending my life, I turned myself into the police.

Daly City, 2002

Ultimately, it seemed taking my own life was going to involve more evasive measures. I wasn't sure what act would end my life. By this time, I relied heavily on alcohol to get by. What I didn't know was that alcohol would be the instrument leading to my second arrest and my fourth suicide attempt.

Since I was so heavily dependent on alcohol, it wasn't surprising that my second arrest was a DUI. After a long night of partying in a San Francisco club, I had no issue driving home intoxicated. Of course, the South San Francisco police pulled me over for a spontaneous DUI test. Upon failing, I was immediately arrested and spent the night sobering up in jail.

As for my fourth suicide attempt, it was another miracle I'm shocked to have survived. It was Christmas Eve 2002 and I was going through my second bottle of Hennessy. Driving in my Escalade, I purposefully ran through every red light. I couldn't even remember how many red lights I went through that night but fate…or some higher power…decided that was not my time…again. *"Why can't I just kill myself?"* I thought. With another day to look forward to, I hardly spent it being grateful for yet another chance at life. Surprisingly, someone came into my life out of her own free will, so that maybe, just maybe, I had hope of happier days to come.

CHAPTER 8

The Patient Wife

Daly City, 2003

In the midst of all this chaos in my life, I met Laura. She became my wife and the light that brought peace into my life. Her undeniable inner beauty manifested itself outwardly. I knew this was the relationship that kept me grounded…at least for a little while. While I still had not dealt with much of the anger and bitterness from my previous relationship; Laura sometimes became an outlet to cope with those feelings. Anytime the boys' mother and I had a disagreement; I lashed out at Laura.

My venting became almost violent, and being a kind woman, Laura did her best to encourage peace between the boys' mother and I. And that made me even angrier! "You're in the relationship with me! Why are you taking her side?" was something I frequently asked Laura. I honestly didn't care what her answer was. I mostly needed Laura to fuel the anger I had already built up and I seldom received it. So I resorted to finding comfort in gambling, drinking and drugs.

Part of the risk when I gambled was the amount of debt that had accumulated during my gambling sprees. My earnings weren't enough to compensate for my gambling addiction and that was a huge problem. This got me to a point where people were looking for me to collect the debt I owed them. Around 2004-2005, my gambling addiction increased, mostly because I was completely unemployed during this time. I no longer bowled because my gambling debt prevented me from traveling and paying for tournaments.

Although I had so much pride in Skanlez-Fit, I lost interest in the clothing line. Anyone who knew me saw how dedicated I had been, and so detail conscious that I folded each shirt myself before distributing them to stores. However, it was difficult to manage all the work in addition to paying for the costs of production. Because of this, I was forced to end Skanlez-Fit. This strained my relationship with Laura because I constantly asked her for money to use on drugs, alcohol and gambling. Those times where she refused to enable my poor choices, I lashed out violently to the point where she gave me money just to avoid the verbal abuse.

I didn't acknowledge it at the time, but Laura went through two years of verbal abuse while being in a relationship with me. More than just verbal abuse, my chaotic behaviors weren't ideal for a woman who moved up from Los Angeles to Daly City, and away from all her family. Still, Laura showed so much patience with me. How and why she remained with me, despite how I treated her, left me stunned. I wouldn't find out until later in our marriage the source of her strength to remain.

Amongst the long list of the troubles in my life, I also suffered from severe depression. Between the emotional issues regarding my previous relationship, to my unsuccessful career paths, depression was just another demon that pulled me further down into the pit I had created for myself. To get me out of the pit, I tried to see if I could compete in bowling again. If I even thought of going back to compete again, I would need a little help. Since I had a supply of meth that I was slowly selling, I thought I would try it again to get an edge in competitions. I tried it and signed up for the next regional PBA tournament. On meth, I felt great and bowled pretty well. I got close to cashing, but not close enough. I felt great! I hated how depression made me feel, and meth was the perfect answer to counteract it.

No one, not even Laura, knew at the time that I had been using meth recreationally. For a while I smoked meth on the weekends just for fun. Most days I relied on marijuana, alcohol and muscle relaxers to get me by. But the more I used meth, the more I wanted, and the more trouble followed me. Because

I used meth so frequently, it became difficult for me to sleep at night. Somehow, I believed mixing alcohol, marijuana, and muscle relaxers were the answer to sleep deprivation after a long day of meth use. However, this mixture may have been the cause of why I frequently and randomly blacked out. While blacked out, I did the craziest things that would put others and myself in danger.

The morning after one of my blackouts, I woke up to a very disturbed look on Laura's face. That usually meant something bad had happened.

"Did something happen again last night?" I asked.

"You started yelling at everyone in the house, rode off with your son's pocket bike, fired your gun in the air and started to kick every garbage can on the street," she replied.

To my disbelief, I ran outside and sure enough, I saw three blocks worth of trashcans knocked down on the street. I wasn't aware how reckless my behavior was when I mixed all these drugs. While this was not one of my better moments, the worst was yet to come. I had hoped that a new relationship with Laura would create a clean slate for my life. However, I still had not dealt with all my other problems. I preferred blaming my problems on my ex, my family, the drugs, the gambling, and even Laura! When in reality, the source of these was myself.

CHAPTER 9

One Dark Destruction After Another

Daly City, 2005

A few weeks after that blackout incident, I admitted my need for psychological help and was willing to see a therapist. I walked in with my family one Monday afternoon, anxious about what would happen in the next hour. During the therapy session, Laura, my parents and I agreed I needed some type of medication that would inhibit my depressed feelings and psychotic behaviors. Obviously, the solutions I relied on caused me to act recklessly. My hope was that whatever medication the doctor prescribed would be able to prevent episodes like these from happening again.

Unfortunately, the psychiatrist wanted a second opinion before he prescribed me any medication. By this time not only had my family felt something bad was going to happen again, but I also felt it. Therefore, I pleaded with the doctor to prescribe me something that day before I left. However, the doctor persisted in getting a second opinion. Well, three nights later, something did happen.

This time, my blacking out did not result in me waking up in my own bed. In fact, where I slept was not a bed at all, but a very cold concrete bench in the county jail. When I woke up, it felt like a nightmare. I was in disbelief that this was real, and started to yell out loudly, "Where am I? How did I get here?" Somehow I found the sense to request a phone call and call my house. That was when my mom answered the phone and explained how I got into county jail. What seemed to be all a dream began with an evening in a San Francisco nightclub. Mom told me I started a fight with the bouncers of the club. They were trying to escort me out because of my drunken behavior.

While my friends were trying to drag me back towards the parking lot and to the car, I started to punch and break every car window that I passed by. Now, I wasn't just angry with the bouncers of the club; I was angry with my friends for not allowing me to act out my anger towards the bouncers. So then, as my friends drove me home, I started to punch my friend, who was driving. While punching him throughout the entire drive home, which takes about 25 minutes, my friend had to stop at a shopping center five blocks short from my house. This is when I ran into a local pub and started trouble there.

I grabbed anything I could throw at parked cars. It wasn't long before the entire South San Francisco police department surrounded, grabbed, cuffed, and placed me in the back of a police vehicle.

That's all I remember my mom telling me as I passed out on the cold concrete bench. It felt like everything she told me about that night was a dream, a bad dream. And, as I woke up from this terrible dream, I still remained in the same jail cell. Eventually, I came to the realization that everything mom told me was true. Although it was true, today, I still don't remember a thing that happened that night. Ironically, this third arrest was in the same exact location as my DUI arrest.

My older brother drove up as soon as he heard I was in jail, to bail me out. At this time, he lived in Riverside, California. After Armando bailed me out, he and my family drove me back to the same doctor who saw me before this incident. After I explained to the doctor the events that had occurred these past couple of days, he prescribed me anti-depressant pills. The medication definitely helped me remain a little more calm, though maybe just a little *too* calm. The anti-depressants would make me sleep for most of the day, and when I woke up, I often felt like a zombie. I remember this one time when I was sitting with my kids on the couch. As they stared at me, I was staring at the TV, until I fell into a deep sleep. This was my usual behavior.

I had the medication for a month and after the pills were gone, I had no desire to refill my prescription. The medication made me feel even more depressed. Since I didn't have medical insurance at that time, I justified that we could not afford to keep paying for the medication. Eventually, I convinced my family that I would be fine without the anti-depressants. I was fine, for a while. What they didn't know was I had started to use meth again. This took my recreational use of meth to an abusive level.

Although meth was a way to alleviate depression in my life by giving me much more energy; it eventually made me act out very violently. At this point of my life, my reckless behavior forced my friends to want nothing to do with me. I lost the trust of my family and friends, and even my children were afraid to be around me. This all resulted in another crazy moment. It happened at Skyline Elementary School, on another foggy, cold day (let's be real here, that's 90% of the days and nights in Daly City).

That day, I was out on the playground alone. This was unusual because whenever I took off, people would go look for me. But this time, no one was looking. That's when I had this crazy idea. *"If I go back home hurt, then everyone would feel bad they didn't look for me, because I came home hurt."* My intention was that those around me would pay attention to me all the time so nothing "bad" would happen.

I went with this thought and walked over to 7-11. I bought a 40 oz. beer, drank it, broke it and started hitting myself with the bottle on my head over and over again until I saw blood coming out. I came home screaming as loudly and frantically as I possibly could. When my wife and mom woke up, they asked me what happened. I told them a bogus story about how I got beat up by some random guys. My goal was to get the attention I needed, and hoped this would cause them to pay attention to me more often.

All the while, Laura stuck by me patiently and lovingly, despite the hell I put her through. One of the worst parts about this time was that my own family kept trying to convince Laura to leave me. She should have, especially after the next incident. I had one of my episodes again and threatened to drive Laura's car off the Golden Gate Bridge. This wasn't a suicide attempt, I had just gotten so upset with the attacks against me. However this time, Laura had the police over to the house while she packed all of her stuff to leave me and move back to Southern California *for good*. Upon hearing this, I immediately calmed down and promised my wife I'd never yell at her or go crazy again. Though I still used meth heavily, I maintained a calmer temperament from that point on in my relationship with Laura.

That was when I met a friend, who for privacy's sake, I'll call Roger. Eventually, I ran out of my own supply of meth that

I had used to sell. So, I turned to one of my customers to see if he had other connections to buy drugs. He introduced me to Roger, who became a friend. This may sound weird, because it probably is, but he taught me how to use meth. I basically went through an interview before he sold me some drugs. He asked me questions like: how do you smoke it, how much do you smoke, and how often do you smoke?

After his assessment, he explained to me I'd been using meth the wrong way (as if there was a right way!). Well, I found out there was a better way. Roger taught me the correct way to smoke meth, and how to spread out my smoking sessions. He also only sold me two weeks' worth of meth at a time. So, when I would go to him short of two weeks, he would get upset with me, and not sell me any more because I was over using the supply. These were the times I would probably act up at home because I couldn't get my fix for a few days.

That was when I had to look for "an in-between" supplier. This supplier would fill in the gaps, when I wasn't buying from Roger. The only issue was, not all methamphetamine is the same. This addiction started to take a toll on my body and mind. For the next year, this would be my pattern, one that I thought I would be following for the rest of my life. Why do I mention this story about my friend Roger? I wanted you to meet him in my story because just one month prior to August 9, 2006, he told me something that later became a reality in my life.

During a long smoking session at Roger's house he turned to me and another younger man and said, "You know, one day you guys are not going to need this anymore." I really didn't know what he meant, or understood why a grown man, who'd been smoking and selling drugs for the past twenty years, told two young men we didn't need to smoke meth anymore. That was when I thought Roger was going crazy. Why would he encourage two of his customers to stop smoking meth?

At this point, I had decided that meth would be a part of my life for the rest of it. But, for some reason, I felt some truth in what he said. I thanked him, "Thanks man, I think I really needed to hear that." But, in the meantime, we just kept on smoking and getting high all day long.

After long sessions of smoking with Roger, I would go home in a great and positive mood. Since I was unemployed, I used most of my free time cleaning the house and fixing things. Most important, I stopped getting mad, yelling at my wife and was somewhat peaceful. But, I also wondered how long it would last; likewise, I think my wife wondered the same thing.

CHAPTER 10

Through the Eyes of The Patient Wife

O ver the next few weeks, conversations between us had seemed calmer, and with a sense of *awkward* stillness. Rocky wasn't yelling at me any longer. Although you would think I would be ecstatic, I sensed that he was still struggling, and because he was unable to let out his frustrations verbally, something began eating him up inside. Although I grew up in a Christian home, I didn't really have much more knowledge about Christianity than what I was taught. My mother always encouraged me to pray and hope. Pray to God, I knew. But the hope part was still a mystery. Yet, prayer provided me with a sense that all would be okay, along with unending peace… something I desperately needed.

I believed that's a big part of why I tolerated the verbal abuse. All those times that Rocky had been yelling, I pretended to use the bathroom. If he only knew — on the other side of the door was his wife on her knees pleading to God in prayer for a way out of this difficult time in our marriage. I prayed I'd be able to give my utmost self as his wife until either it was time for me to leave, or Rocky would kill himself. *God have mercy on me.* The last part of my prayer saddened me, even if it was just a passing thought, and perhaps that too kept me where God wanted me to be. Regardless, through my pleading, God revealed Himself in unfathomable ways and in my heart. God kept saying, *"Laura just love him."* So, I did just that.

Every so often, friends, family and loved ones that knew what was happening in our personal life asked *"Why do you stay?"* I didn't have an answer that they would be familiar with, or accept. But, I knew that there was something inside Rocky that desired to overcome this chaos. THAT gave me hope. Hope he would fight whatever we were going through. It was a hope I truly didn't fully understand, that was to be revealed at a later time.

I recall a few times when I asked Rocky if we could attend church, and he would be quick to reply, *"No."* He hated church. During this time of calm stillness, Rocky always kept busy and loved to occupy his mind by reading. He also didn't ask me for money like he used to. Perhaps his desires were gone, or he was tired of asking, I wasn't really sure. But, soon thereafter, Rocky asked if he might have some money for Barnes & Noble — this was new. I always desired to encourage any good within him, so I willingly and happily gave him money for this.

He often came back home with an actual book (sometimes books), which made me smile because that brought me more hope. He bought books that focused on change, encouragement, and self-motivation. For weeks he continued going and sharing good books from popular spiritual authors. And though I tried to share God, I ceased because it wasn't well received. However, I continued just loving him. Then, when things seemed to be getting better, there was a halt in our progress.

I remember that night so clearly. It was a cold foggy night in Daly City. Sound familiar? Whatever the conversation that stirred Rocky to be riled up inside, I don't remember, but this was the end of his calm behavior, and the last straw for me. My body was physically drained. My mind was mentally exhausted and though I never threatened to leave, except to protect him (like the Golden Gate-Bridge incident), God knew in my heart that I was done. I told Rocky I was tired, and he knew that it meant more than just being physically tired. He knew that it was the end of the line for me. So, in his dismay before he would begin to yell and verbally abuse me, he forced himself to leave, and walked outside alone and upset. At this point, I didn't know where the night would lead…

SECTION 4

AND SO BEGINS THE SPIRITUAL JOURNEY

"The wind blows where it wishes and you hear its sound, but you do not know where it goes."

John 3:8 [ESV]

CHAPTER 11

Redemption on the broken road (Night of August 9th, 2006)

"I'm tired," she said.

Her words were so simple…yet carried so much meaning. How could I go off and yell at Laura again? I thought everything was starting to get better. At least, it definitely seemed that way. I honestly believed all those self-help books had sunk in and changed something within me. I would become a better husband and father to my family. But I guess I was wrong.

As I walked outside of our house on Gellert Blvd., and sat down on the cold cement floor at my next-door neighbor's garage door; I felt the weight of all these past years fall back on my shoulders. I couldn't take it anymore, and my family deserved way better than me. All these pains I had been carrying couldn't be fixed by anything! What was left to help me? There was only one solution I could think of. I didn't know how I was going to attempt suicide this time, but I knew for sure it would be the last time, despite my previous failed attempts.

Yet, in the midst of all this anger and frustration, I went from sitting down to falling on my knees and crying out to the sky, *"God, if you're there, please help me. I don't want to hurt myself; I don't want to hurt my wife and anyone else anymore. Please change me God."* As soon as I said that, I felt this peace that began flowing through my body like I had never felt before — a feeling like a 100 apes came off my back. I felt in my heart God telling me, "Rocky, I've always been here. As long as you put me first in your life…you'll be just fine." I wasn't sure what God meant by putting Him first, but I was on my way to figuring out how that was going to work in my life.

Like before, I felt things were going to get better, but I didn't know how long it would last. Was this peace going to leave me again? Despite my uncertainty, I did know that something about crying out to God had to do with this peace, and I wanted to know more about Him…who He was, where He came from, etc. So, I ran upstairs into the room where Laura was. I was still unsure of the moments that happened before, but I knew my wife had seen a different person.

***

LAURA'S UNEXPECTED SURPRISE

Laura speaks:

Once Rocky left the house, I really didn't know what I to expect when he came back. I was sitting in our room, on the bed watching TV. Honestly, I don't remember what was on or what I was thinking about. After what seemed longer than 10 minutes, I heard footsteps coming down the hall towards the room. I knew who it was, and was ready for whatever was to come. Whether it was the usual yelling, or whether he came back with an absurd story of someone attacking him outside and returning with some odd cuts and scrapes, my heart became anxious and, as usual I became numb thinking of what to say…

Rocky quickly entered the room and for some reason, he had this interesting glow on his face. He was out of breath, not like someone who was tired, but like someone who was anxious and excited. It was an unrecognizable glow. That's the best I could explain it then, and even now. Basically, he looked different and truly happy. I waited anxiously for something to come out of his mouth.

"I don't know what happened," Rocky replied.

"What do you mean, you don't know what happened?" I said. I was trying to be very careful with my words in this unfamiliar territory.

Rocky explained, "Okay, I went outside very angry and ready to kill myself, and as I sat outside thinking of what I was going to do or how I was going to do it, I began to cry and looked up in the sky and said, *'God, if you're there, please help me. I don't want to hurt myself; I don't want to hurt my wife and anyone else anymore. Please change me God.'* Immediately after I was done, I felt this overwhelming sense of peace that I have never felt before, and I felt as if this burden was lifted off of me. I felt at peace. I don't know what happened."

I quickly responded, "Wow, that sounds like God heard you and gave you the Holy Spirit." My quick response was due to what my parents taught me, though I didn't know what it truly meant at the time. But I knew this moment was what my parents had told me about. I was in awe, and replayed that moment in my mind over and over again. Then we just talked about what happened and we didn't know what to do with it. The days, weeks and months ahead unraveled the amazing things that were to come.

CHAPTER 12

Persistent Search

"If we find ourselves with a desire that nothing in this world can satisfy, the most probable explanation is that we were made for another world."

C.S. Lewis

hree days later (August 12th), Laura and I went over to Minda's house. I went down to the garage to play on the drums for a little bit (more like beating the drum head). Anyway, while drumming high and happy on meth, Laura had been telling Minda about the changes she's seen in my character since that night of August 9th. Even though I was still using meth regularly, there was still this change of character that my family noticed, especially when I began searching for God. Three days seemed like a short period of time to me for changes to be noticeable. But, I guess I was so much of a mess, that any change of behavior was an obvious one. I really didn't have the desire to change. I only focused on finding the God I was supposed to put first. Maybe that's why I didn't bother trying to stop smoking meth or stop any of the other things I was addicted to. However, soon enough, there would be more addiction behavior that would go away as I persistently pursued God.

***

LAURA AND MINDA'S CONVERSATION

Laura speaks:

My hope was strengthened and I felt that God had heard my prayers. Yet, I felt so undeserving in the days that followed. I knew God heard me after each verbal abuse incident…especially the times I pleaded with a heavy heart in the bathroom. I recall many nights and early mornings when my eyes grew heavy, until Rocky yelled himself to sleep. I hoped I would be able to sneak in a couple of hours of rest before work, and then make my way out quietly. After August 9th, those days and evenings seemed to fade away.

Rocky's family heard of the changes that were happening within him and although they were glad, they also remained skeptical, since this was a common pattern in his life. However, I knew something was different this time…something genuine and very real. We were on our way to hang out with the family at Minda's house when she heard about the changes with Rocky. She was very happy to hear that her little brother was trying to better himself, for himself and his family. As I sat across from Minda in the upstairs living room, I shared the amazing changes that were happening in our lives, though I wasn't truly able to explain how it was happening.

In the middle of describing these changes to Minda, she suggested, "Hey, why don't you guys go to church with us?" It was a great idea, but I surprised myself by saying, "I think that would be good, but the way things have been happening lately, let's wait for him to mention it. I don't want to rush him into it." Minda agreed, and we decided we would wait for him to ask about church.

As soon as we finished our discussion, Rocky came upstairs and asked, "Hey Min, you guys going to church tomorrow?" I don't know about Minda, but my jaw dropped in awe! Minda and I looked at each other then laughed. Rocky looked a little confused and was eyeing us both.

"What happened?" Rocky asked.

I explained what Minda and I had just talked about, and how amazing it was that he quickly confirmed our plan.

***

Since that day was Saturday, I went to church with my family the following day. Although I had been raised in a Catholic home, this was the first time I really wanted to attend church. I remember back in the day, my family and I would always get to mass late. From the time I was 9 years old, Armando and I would grab some of the bulletins with the advertisements in the back and make paper airplanes. We were so much into making them that we'd sneak outside to see whose plane would fly the longest. This is probably my greatest memory of Catholic Church (aside from all the baptisms I saw).

I felt good being at mass after such a long time, but something just didn't feel right. The message was good, but I knew I had to attend church more and more to complete my search for the God I cried out to. While I was determined to know more about this God, I still didn't have any intention of giving up any of my old vices.

However, they seemed to go away by themselves, almost every day. That afternoon after mass, I went to grab a beer with my brother-in-law. For some strange reason the beer wasn't as satisfying as before. Without knowing it, this would be the last time I would drink alcohol. The other weird thing that was changing was my language. I used to say a lot of bad words, but now my mouth was being cleaned up. The changes were all strange to me, but I didn't give it much attention until a few days later.

CHAPTER 13

Victory of Meth

August 17th, just eight days after I cried out to God, was the last time I'd ever smoke meth. Around that time, I was doing about six sessions of meth per day. As I was smoking my first session of the day, I couldn't seem to get a high. So I kept smoking until I ran out of supply, which was two weeks' worth of meth. Surprisingly, with all that meth in my system, I experienced no high. I realized there was probably a reason why it wasn't working this time. But, looking back, I think there was still a part of me that wanted to be okay with getting high.

A week later, I got angry and frustrated again, which was a result of withdrawal from meth. I called Laura hoping she was able to calm me down. Although her words were encouraging, I continued to be angry and frustrated to the point where I hung up on her. After, I was determined to get ahold of some meth and smoke it. But instead of making the phone call right away, I prayed.

"God, after I pray this prayer, I'm gonna go buy meth and smoke it. If I don't need it in my life anymore, take it away." I said my Amen, went straight to my cell phone, and called my most reliable source. Just in case you're not familiar with how drug addicts work, let me just say that every addict always has a backup plan to a reliable source. Usually, your reliable source is your "go to" person because there is barely any gap in time between when you call and receive the drugs.

With that said, I called Reliable Source #1. Usually, this person picks up and if he misses the call, he always calls back. After no answer, I called about ten more times, yet still no luck. I then proceeded to call Reliable Source #2. After two rings, he picks up his phone and automatically asks how he can help me. However, it turned out he happened to be in Disneyland with his family! I took it as a sign, wished him a great vacation and hung up the phone.

I took these calls as a sign that God had been listening to my prayer, and that I didn't need drugs in my life. After a quick "thanks" to God, all I could think about were the meth pipes I still had. As soon as I got to the garage, the first things I grabbed were the pipes and then I smashed each one with my foot. Crushing them to pieces felt exhilarating, because this would be the last time I would ever have the urge to smoke meth. It was still a couple of hours before Laura would come home. I kept myself busy by cleaning the garage, waiting for her.

When Laura got home, apparently she felt I needed something more than just a few words of encouragement. To my surprise, she arrived with a cake and a card. That simple act of support led to a great evening — an evening where the events beforehand would have to remain secret. But, that's because up to this point, Laura had been in the dark about my meth use. However, the events of this night would reveal themselves in the months to come.

SECTION 4

A REFUGE FROM THE STORM

CHAPTER 14

Where is God?

"And there is salvation in no one else, for there is no other name under heaven given among men by which we must be saved"

Acts 4:12 (ESV)

"Be careful when you pursue truth, because you just might find him."

Jefferson Bethke

As I kept going to the Catholic Church, I continued my search for the God I cried out to. In the Catholic Church, I found myself going through the motions. Going to church every Sunday, saying the Lord's Prayer daily, confessing my sins to a priest, etc. To sum it all up, I exhausted everything the Catholic Church had to give me just to find the God I had to place first in my life. It seemed like my new turn in life spread around like wildfire, because everyone who knew "the old me" heard about the changes that were happening and wanted to help motivate me to continue going in the right direction. My sons' great grandma heard about my interest in God, and gave me the main resource that taught me about Jehovah Witness. Although I was very interested in the book, their view of Jesus was not something I was familiar with, so I continued my search.

During this time, I casually stumbled upon a conversation amongst two Mormons (or rather, they stumbled upon me). I was just playing basketball with my two sons outside the house, when I saw two nicely dressed young men approaching me wearing gold nametags. I didn't know what to think when these guys walked over to me. But I had a habit at looking at people who wore nametags so I could call them by their name. On both of their nametags, it said "Elder."

So I asked, "Oh, both of your names are Elder?"

I know it sounds like I was being sarcastic, but it was a serious question. Both men were kind enough to let me know "elder" showed their position in the Mormon Church (which kind of showed how much I really knew about all that "church stuff"). Speaking of church stuff, they started to share with me what they did at their church. Seeing as how they came in the middle of me spending time with my children, they were kind enough to ask me if I was free on another day to talk more about Mormonism.

"Sure, come back tomorrow," I said.

They came back the next day to sit and talk with me at my dining room table. The more they talked about their Jesus, the more I saw that their Jesus wasn't the same one I was taught about. I still wasn't sure yet about Mormonism. However, the two young men invited me to their church to play ball and walk me through their facilities. I remember going to the church with Darien, and while I was there; I ran into a lot of other Westmoor guys I had gone to school with. (Judging by the people there, I had a feeling they were invited to the church by the same guys I talked to.) What I liked most about these people was that they really made me, a stranger, feel welcome. Because of their outstanding hospitality, I strongly considered joining the Mormon Church...especially when they said I could give my testimony.

That aspect was really important to me, because I was really excited about sharing the changes taking place from who I was before August 9th, 2006, to the person I was becoming. I still was not sure if the god of the Mormons was the one I needed to find, so I put Mormonism in the back of my mind and kept searching.

One of the religions I studied most was the fastest growing: Islam. I would pick up the kids at school and found out Darien had a friend that practiced fasting. It turned out Darien's friend was Muslim. So, I asked him if he had any reading material about the Quran. By this time I had developed a desire to read more and more. So, he let me borrow the resources he had about Islam. I remember when I took it home to read, my dad got mad at me for reading about Muslims. What I read changed my perspective on their religion. As I continued reading about the Quran and Islam, I learned they were a very peaceful group of people. But, nothing I read pushed me to want to move forward with practicing Islam.

Sometime after, I ran into a friend at the bowling center. I began telling him the story of how I suddenly lost the desire to smoke meth. He responded by saying that the drugs will always be in my system, however, there's a process I can go through to eliminate the drugs in my body. As he talked about this process, he mentioned it was connected to a religion called Scientology.

The process of removing drugs really didn't interest me much because I knew I was done with drugs. But, when he said "religion" I was interested, because religion to me meant it involved a god. So, I asked him more about Scientology, and he explained that anyone from any religious background could join Scientology. As he kept talking about Scientology, the more it sounded cultish. So I listened for a while, trying to end the subject. I let him share a bit more, but eventually I just went on my way.

I found New Age religion to be the most interesting out of all the religions as I searched for the God I was looking to put first in my life. The New Age movement was the most interesting because it didn't force me to believe one way is better than another. New Age referenced a lot of Buddhism, Hinduism, and even Jesus. I first became interested in the New Age movement when I purchased self-help books at B&N. As I mentioned before, the more I read them, the more I felt at peace. By this time, I'd read perhaps 30 books about the New Age movement, and each book started to sound more and more like the others.

Around Christmas time, I came across a book that had a similar title to another New Age book I had. So, I bought the book for myself as a Christmas present. Little did I know that this was far from a New Age book.

CHAPTER 15

The Spirit Leading Me

S ince the book was a Christmas present for me, I actually waited until the holiday came to open it. The book was set up as a 40-day read, which meant I would read one section of the book for the next 40 days. So, I thought it was the perfect book to start in the New Year.

Over the course of my reading, I began to see why God created humankind and our purpose for being on this earth. On February 9th 2007, day 40, I finally completed the book. The final suggestion for having a purpose-driven life was to find a Bible-teaching church. *Another item to search for?* I still wasn't sure what God I was supposed to follow, let alone know what a Bible-teaching church was. However, everything in the book up to that point had been very helpful. So, if a Bible-teaching church was the next step to having a better life, then you'd better believe I wanted to find one.

I honestly did not know where to start, or how I could find one. Coincidentally (again…I would find out later there's no such thing as coincidence), I was overdue for a dental appointment, so Laura scheduled me for an appointment at a dental office near the Century 20 Theater in Daly City. After visiting this office, I was annoyed by the visit, and asked Laura if she could find me another dentist. Eventually, she scheduled an appointment for me with Dr. Legaspi (whose office at the time was just down the street from our house on Gellert Boulevard). After several X-rays, Dr. Legaspi discovered how bad my teeth were. As she explained the poor condition of my teeth, I couldn't help but tell her why my teeth were so bad, and why I had taken such poor care of them (mostly due to how heavily involved I was with drugs). Eventually, I began to tell her what God had been doing recently in my life.

I mentioned that I was searching for a Bible-teaching church. She mentioned that the church she attended is a non-denominational church in the San Bruno area.

"What's the name of the church?" I asked.

Dr. Legaspi replied, "Church of the Highlands."

Since the church was located near work, I made sure I would check it out the next time I was in the area. Two weeks passed by, but I still had not made any attempt to attend Church of the Highlands.

Coincidentally, *again*, I stopped by Classic Bowl to hang out with a few buddies of mine. At this point, I just wanted to tell everyone about all the changes that were going on in my life. I began by just sharing my stories with the friends who were there. At the end, I mentioned again that I was looking for a Bible-teaching church. Two of my friends, Freddy and Lina Cooper suggested I attend their church.

"What church do you go to?" I asked.

And you would not believe what *their* answer was: Church of the Highlands. This was definitely not coincidence, something…rather someone…was guiding me to this place. Yet, after one month had gone by, I still had not set foot into Church of the Highlands.

CHAPTER 16

The Truth That Set Me Free

"It wasn't an intellectual or even an emotional connection, it was a connection of our wills."

Jim Stump

March had arrived and my 30th birthday was coming up. The memories of telling my family that I would never live to see the age of 30, rushed through my mind. By this time, my family and I had moved to a new location. The significance of this move, to a new location off Skyline Blvd., was to avoid the post-work evening traffic jam. I avoided taking Highway 280 N. Instead, I would take Sneath Lane towards Skyline Blvd.

Coincidentally, I frequently passed a sign that read "Church of the Highlands," which was on the corner of Sneath Lane and Skyline Blvd. Every time I passed that sign, I often told myself that I would go in and see that church. Two different people had already mentioned that this could be the church I was looking for. But, even after two weeks of avoiding traffic to make my way home, I had not attended a single service at Church of the Highlands.

Finally, the weekend before my 30th birthday, I took the initiative by telling my family that we were going to attend church this weekend at Church of the Highlands. I was so excited that my family and I went early so that we could get seats in the front. While we were waiting to go inside, I saw an old friend (in a suit) walk into the church office. I followed him to say hello and also wanted to share the amazing changes that were happening in my life. Seeing someone that I knew was cool, and a confirmation that God had been leading us here the whole time.

Once we were able to enter the church service, I rushed my family to the front row near the piano. While waiting for the service to start, Pastor Donald Sheley welcomed my family and I to church. I didn't realize at the time that he was the founding pastor. Our first time there turned out to be a great experience not only for myself, but also my family. For me, I enjoyed how they read and explained the section of the Bible the pastor focused on.

It was enjoyable for Laura because she was raised with a Christian background and the worship aspect of the service was similar to what she grew up with. Because the service we attended was a youth-led service (which means the high school youth pastor led the sermon), Darien and Nathaniel liked the fact they got to hear a sermon that catered to their age group. Since our first time was such a positive experience, I definitely wanted to return the following week.

Before I left, this guy Ted Melendez, handed me a bible and suggested I read through the Gospel of John. Being the enthusiastic reader I was, I finished the book of John without much difficulty. However, I did not fully understand what I read, so I read it again. The second time through, as I got to the eighth chapter, I felt that God was speaking to my heart. The verse that caught my attention was verse 32. Jesus says, "the truth will set you free."

This whole time, I'd been searching everywhere for the truth. And at this point in my reading, I think I finally found it. The truth was: the God I had been searching for was Jesus. Jesus, the One who died on the cross for all of my sins, and who proved that He was God by raising himself up from the dead. From this moment, moving forward, it is Jesus I'm supposed to put first in my life.

To tell you the truth, I didn't fully understand everything at that point, and I still don't understand everything written in the bible. However, then I knew for sure that for the rest of my life, I would try my best to learn more about Jesus and what he truly means in my life. The night of August 9th, God started to make tremendous physical and mental changes that were obvious to everyone. But, when I realized it was Jesus I was supposed to put first, I started to notice God was changing my heart too. Then I asked, "What's next?"

The following weekend, my family wanted to celebrate my 30th birthday on Sunday, March 25th. I really wanted to go back to Church of the Highlands, so I decided to go to the Saturday night service by myself (which was my actual birthday), as the boys were with their mom, and Laura worked every Saturday. That Saturday evening, it was Pastor Leighton that gave the evening message. At the end of his message, he gave an invitation to accept Jesus Christ as your personal Lord and Savior.

He asked the congregation, "If anyone would like to do that, with everyone's eyes closed, would you raise your hand." So, I raised my hand. All this time, I'd been telling people of the changes that had been going on my life since August 9th, 2006; about the night I wanted to end my life, but instead I cried out for God to change me. And that's when God spoke in my heart, that as long as I put Him first…I'd be fine. Finally, on my 30th birthday…it's not that I found God (because He was never lost), it was that I finally realized He was always there and His name is Jesus.

For the next few weeks, I joined every available bible study group that Church of the Highlands offered. I couldn't get enough of God's Word. All of a sudden, I started to under-stand more of it, which meant a growing knowledge about Jesus. But, I also knew I wouldn't get ahead, or at least learn fast, without surrounding myself with other godly men: men who reflected God's love in their life by the way they loved their wife, children and others. The more I started to learn, the knowledge I gained gave me more zeal to tell people about Christ. Soon enough, I would get my chance to share my story, and the result of that opportunity was something I could have never imagined.

CHAPTER 17

New Life

Two months later, on Mother's Day, I had the opportunity to tell my story in front of the congregation. I also had an opportunity to invite my family members, including my mom. That morning would be the first time my family members would hear about some of the things I had been struggling with in the past few years. Most of them were not aware of my drug addiction until that Sunday morning.

A few of my old friends and family members that had been hurt by me, showed up to hear my testimony, and I had an opportunity to ask for forgiveness for the first time. It was an amazing morning being able to tell my story of a transformed life. But, something even more amazing happened that day. Laura too raised her hand and accepted Jesus into her heart for the very first time.

***

Laura speaks:

Ever experience a scene as in a movie, where you're in a room, surrounded by many people, and all of a sudden you flashback to a place where you're all alone, all the while seeing that you're not? A place where all the noise is silent and you see all the faces in the room, as if you're looking at all of them from the perspective of a fly on the wall.

As Rocky was giving his testimony to the congregation, my life reeled like a fast forward movie. My thoughts raced, and I asked myself, "Laura, you see the miraculous work that God is doing in Rocky's life, right? You grew up as a Christian, but did you ever commit your life to Him? What does it take to make you see that? Do you need to go through something that drastic in order to make you realize this? Or will you follow that tug that's in your heart? Don't you want the same joy that you see in your husband's "new" life?

I was plagued with question after question. Then it hit me like an ocean swallowing up my heart...I want all of that! Yes, God, I want a relationship with you. But what does that mean? The moment these questions ran through my mind, I found myself back again to being in church. All the familiar faces and noises began to fill my senses back up again. Then, I heard Pastor Leighton giving an altar call. "If you have not yet received Jesus Christ as your Lord and Savior, this is the time to do so." I found myself in God's presence within a room full of people, but I felt as if God was talking to me alone, helping me answer those questions I'd never taken the time to ask. "Yes, Lord, I don't know what that means, but I trust you will help me to understand. I want you and plead for you to come into my heart, my life, and be Master of it. Amen."

***

I'm not sure about you, but what is greater than telling your church, family and friends about God saving your life? While I was telling my salvation story, God was working in Laura's heart at that very moment to grant her the same gift of salvation He had given me! Has everything been perfect since I became a Christian? No! Did I suddenly stop struggling and my life became problem free? No! All I know is that my life has been full of joy. My life is a lot more peaceful and definitely full of hope. Hope, not in my wife or myself, rather hope in my God, that one day I will be with Him forever in a perfect place! I write my story now, not for the sake of selling books, but to convey my prayer is for you or someone you know, who is capable of having that *same* hope as I have today.

Speaking of today, as I reflect on these words, God has blessed my wife and I with beautiful twin girls (Neriah Grace and Eliana Faith). I have been ordained as a Pastor at Church of the Highlands for youth ministry. I recently graduated from Liberty University with a bachelor's degree in Biblical Studies and Christian Counseling. As I finish up this book, my prayer is to continue to share with people other aspects of my life through stories. Since the night of August 9, 2006, there is still a burning desire to continue to tell me story of a transformed life.

I have no idea how this book will do, or if anyone is ever going to be impacted by it. But, what I do know is God only told me to put Him first, and by putting Him first, He will do the rest. The Apostle Paul wrote, "Work out your salvation with fear and trembling; for it is God who is at work in you, both to will and to work for His good pleasure" (Phil. 2:12-13(ESV)).

A few years ago, I shared with and reminded my wife, how for five years; I told everyone that I would die before I reached the age of 30. Laura replied, "In fact, you did die at the age of 30, but not the way you expected. When you accepted Jesus Christ as your personal Lord and Savior, your old self died and now you are alive in Christ." For the bible says, "I have been crucified with Christ. It is no longer I who live, but Christ who lives in me. And the life I now live in the flesh I live by faith in the Son of God, who loved me and gave himself for me" (Gal. 2:20 (ESV)).

For most of my life I have lived for myself and tried to fulfill my own desires. But, this entire time the life I'm supposed to live is a life putting God first, and everyone else next.

Afterword

For the Reader

If this book is for you, you are going through something similar, and you are exhausted with being tired, sick of your life, and have nowhere else to turn — I encourage you to cry out to God. Cry out to Him and let Him take your worries and leave the results in His hands. So, if you want to do that right now, please repeat this prayer:

> *God, if you're there, I'm sick of my life. Would you please change me?*
> *Come into my life and help me put you first. I don't exactly know what to do after this, but I know you will guide me. Amen!*

If you just prayed this, I would love to hear from you so please contact me at:

Email: Arnaldo.Concepcion@gmail.com
Address: 1900 Monterey Drive, San Bruno, CA 94066
Phone: 650-266-4372

Or go to the nearest Bible-teaching church in your area and ask for the Pastor to help guide you to your new life in Christ.

If you are a wife, mother or friend that has someone in mind, and you are searching for hope and haven't found any, please pray this:

Lord Jesus, I know you are God and I know with you all things are possible. Please change [name] and reveal to him/her who you really are. Please use me as an instrument of peace and love to show [name] there is hope in you as long as he/she puts you first in his/ her life. Amen!

Likewise, if you prayed this prayer, I would love to hear from you, and be able to pray with or for you. So, please reach me by using the information above. Now that you have finished reading this book, "Rocky: A Life Transformed", please go out and share it with others.

Closing Prayer:

LORD JESUS, THANK YOU FOR BEING MY GOD. MY PRAYER IS FOR THOSE THAT ARE READING THIS TODAY, THAT THEY WILL PUT YOU FIRST IN THEIR LIVES. ALTHOUGH WE MAY STILL CONTINUE TO STRUGGLE IN CERTAIN AREAS OF OUR LIVES, WE WILL PERSIST TO FOCUS NOT ON THE THINGS OF THIS WORLD, BUT TO FOCUS ON YOU, BY ALWAYS PUTTING YOU FIRST! I PRAY THESE THINGS TO MY GOD, MY LORD AND SAVIOR JESUS CHRIST . . .AMEN!

THE END
OF A NEW BEGINNING

From the Co-Author

L ike many of you, this story of overcoming one's greatest struggles and finding an everlasting peace really resonated with me. When I first met Arnaldo [Rocky], I expected he had a past…just like everyone else I knew. The more I got to know him, the more he shared the struggles he had dealt with before having a relationship with Christ.

It wasn't even until we started writing this book that I truly saw the power in his testimony. One of my first reactions was, "You should've died." As you read his story, there were many times he tried to take his own life or that it was at risk. Yet, God had other plans for Arnaldo's life. He used one man's life to impact an eternal change in the lives of others…way before Arnaldo even knew it.

Today, Arnaldo has the pleasure of serving as the Youth Ministry Pastor for our high school students. In the three years he has served as their pastor, he has led many to Christ, challenged the students to live a life of Christ in a society that rejects Christian morals, and has helped educate and raise a generation to go out and speak of the hope that is found in their faith.

In the summer of 2014, our students attended a yearly camp where they spent time building relationships with other churches, and focused some time on their own relationship with God. It was that summer, where Arnaldo truly revealed how much God can "use your mess for His message." It was the first time I've seen him completely vulnerable.

When Arnaldo expressed his acceptance of the things that have happened in his life [despite the pain it caused him], our students were able to tear down the walls that kept Christ from truly coming in and taking hold of their lives. We had 14 students accept Christ as their Lord and Savior that summer. And, even if it was just one student, it was the catalyst our students needed to take a really hard look at their lives.

While our youth ministry has come a long way, much of this would not have been possible without Arnaldo's obedience to God's calling in his life. It began with a broken and weary spirit the night of August 9th, 2006. Never would anyone, let alone Arnaldo, have predicted that this time of chaos could be used to speak life and hope to many of the students that come through our doors each week.

I did not expect that I myself would find hope through his story. And, never would I have expected to have the honor of co-writing this amazing journey of how one's HUGE mess would be used for God's ETERNAL message. May all those who read this story find hope through times of joy and suffering. Hope, not in ourselves, but in a Savior who has granted us the gift of eternal life and happiness in the relationship we have with Him.

Blessings, Jinelle Remo

> *And we know that for those who love God all things work together for the good, for those who are called according to his purpose.*
>
> Romans 8:28 (ESV)